My Molten Wings

My Molten Wings

Sulekha Samantaray

BLACK EAGLE BOOKS
Dublin, USA | Bhubaneswar, India

 Black Eagle Books
USA address:
7464 Wisdom Lane
Dublin, OH 43016

India address:
E/312, Trident Galaxy, Kalinga Nagar,
Bhubaneswar-751003, Odisha, India

E-mail: info@blackeaglebooks.org
Website: www.blackeaglebooks.org

First International Edition Published by
Black Eagle Books, 2025

MY MOLTEN WINGS
by **Sulekha Samantaray**

Copyright © Sulekha Samantaray

All rights reserved. No part of this publication may be reproduced, stored in a retrieval system, or transmitted, in any form or by any means, electronic, mechanical, photocopying, recording or otherwise without the prior permission of the publisher.

Cover & Interior Design: Ezy's Publication

ISBN- 978-1-64560-665-9 (Paperback)

Printed in the United States of America

*Dedicated to my departed parents
with loving regards
for whom I am what I am today.*

CONTENTS

The Snow-capped Mountain	9
Plea to My Pathfinder	10
I am a Sunflower	12
My Molten Wings	13
Time is Running Out	15
Ruminations: 2021	16
Death is Marching	18
Supreme Power	19
Mahalaxmi: Emancipation Incarnated	20
True Contentment	23
Moments to Remember	24
Be A Winged Woman	26
The Wander-Lust Lover	27
In My Prayers	28
Soliloquy of December Flower	30
Rain in March	32
Enigmatic Eyes	34
A Game of Chess	36
Strange Meeting	38
Worth of A Woman	39
Invocation to Maa Ambika	40
Momentary	42
Let's Take A Solemn Pledge	44
From Lamborghini to Chemborghini	46
Another Philomela	48
Power of Camouflaging	50
A Mother: Not Mother-in-law	52
A Victim of Fani	55
A Dream Not Fulfilled	57
The Autumnal Full Moon	59
Fisherman's Wife	60

My Neighbour's Pride	61
Where Are You Anamika	63
A Silver Medal	66
Friendship for Me	67
May Peace Prevail	69
Music of Monitor	70
To My Friend Baruna	71
A Victim's Last Word	73
Play of Chromosomes	74
To My Mother	77
My Laments	79
Come As My Bridegroom	80
Merry in May	81
A Chiselled Marvel	82
No More	84
Masquerade	86
My Tears	88
Something Personal	89
The Pampered Child	90
Come with Your Azure Being	91
Magnanimous Pole Star	93
My Happiness	95
Magic of Malati	96
Forget Me	97
Entice Me Not	99
My Earnest Desires	101
Mysterious Pulchritude	103
A Sanctum of Knowledge	106
The Soul of My Country	108

The Snow Capped Mountain

Standing majestically yonder there
miles away from madding crowds
with shining silvery cap of snow;
The mountain looks shrouded in mystery
that for millenniums was allowed to grow.

No one knows for how many years
the mountain is meditating silently
like self-disciplined ancient sages;
Unperturbed, unmoved by hundreds of
cataclysms that swept the Earth for ages.

What hypnotic power does it possess ?
Which undiscovered treasure does it hide ?
Why are men drawn to it
like a moth to a flame ?
What rewards are assured to men
with this enticement ?

The irresistible desire to climb this mountain,
The unexplained temptation to stand on its cliff,
The overwhelming fascination for this enigma
leads to what kind of fulfilment ?
Is this mountain a reality
or an illusion that vanishes
like a mirage as you come near it ??

Plea to My Path Finder

Beyond the starry firmament
amidst the planetary movement
You are reigning unseen by earthly mortals,
Bless me O' Supreme Artist
with a cultured power of thrift
for building my beatific literary portal.

Beneath your apparent indifference
lies unnoticed bountiful benevolence,
Kindly grant me only fabulous immortal thoughts,
Light up my mind with a spark
of flame divine to dispel the dark
and strengthen my pen making it well-wrought.

Betwixt many ideas wavering
when my pen starts quivering,
Lend me from your studio just one brush,
for I will use that brush as pen
to portray pictures of men and women
their pain, pleasure, struggle, success as a crush.

Before my pen commits any mistake
with ignorance, please be my stake,
Impart your heavenly power with grace abundance,
I want to sing hymns in praise
of you O' God and like to raise voice
for the marginalized, neglected in governance.

Bereft of hope if lazily I sleep
wake me up to enjoy a peep
at the wondrous world filled with novelty,
Gift me the choicest colours
from mystical palette of yours
to paint perpetual word rainbows with majesty.

Behind you my presence I must feel
walking on creative path with zeal,
Kindly act invisibly as my true path finder,
If I halt on a new course
help me by supplying the source
and prod me on ceaselessly with a reminder.

I am a Sunflower

I stand excitedly beside the wide open window,
To welcome my eternal lover, the rising Sun;
I perceive the titillating chilly morning breeze
Arousing in my heart and body a sweet sensation.

Soon the gloomy darkness disappears from east,
The sky is painted with vibrant shades of red and yellow;
Buoyant Apollo ascends with aplomb pouring warm light,
With pleasure I hug the sunshine feeling mellow.

I know not the time when I fell in love, with Sun,
Whose resplendent glory I desire to watch;
Be it morning, noon or evening, I follow him,
Like a Sunflower, no mortal love can be his match.

For me, Sun is not a star nor is he a God,
Full of joy I welcome him daily in the morning,
My tryst with him has countless rendezvouses,
Happily I bid him a transient farewell in the evening.

My Molten Wings

When I was born
I had wings of a dove;
With pearly white delicate feathers,
I used to spread innocent love.

As I grew up, slowly my wings
gathered hues of myriad colours
like the wings of a peacock.
Spreading my rainbow hued feathers,
I danced with the rhythm of rain;
Tantalizing many a heart I sang
the song of youth's mellifluous refrain.

My dream of loving blissfully
in a beautiful Utopian land,
one day turned into reality;
When a prince came on a horse
and whisked me away
to Shangri-La's vicinity.

My fanciful wings
started soaring higher
and higher each day
with novel dreams;
But little did I know
that my dreams would

be short-lived and would
end in fearful screams.

For the tangible reality of life
dyed all the colours of
my wings into molten black,
as they started melting
like the wings of Icarus
and my dream home
suddenly began breaking
like Phaethon's carriage
into pieces, with my distressed
heart silently wailing.

Time is Running Out

With the speed of a supersonic aircraft
Time runs out of the hourglass of life;
All my miserable measures to capture him
turns into Sisyphean tasks, as he chisels
me like a joker with his heartless knife.

Frantically I try to hold back some
fruitful moments in my trembling hands,
but through my incapable fingers
slip out those rare treasures
like powerful waves washing away
my helpless footprints on sands.

I want to paint on the canvas
of my poetic pages some
aesthetically bewitching pictures
before my knell rings.
I wish to tell the untold stories
of my life, opening wide
the locked strong room of mystery;
But sorrowfully I feel
the running time of my journey
reaching the last mile post
dumping me into the debris
of unknown history.

Ruminations: 2021

Let's pray to God and
thank Him for sparing us
from the clutches of Corona.
Let's shed a few drops of
remorseful tears for those innocent
victims of this dreadful disease,
our unfortunate brethren.

Let's remember all those lessons
taught by this pestilential pandemic;
Let's take a pledge to lead
a purified life after
humanity's purgatorial suffering
in the year two thousand twenty.
Let's consciously cultivate
the spirit of penitence in
our daily life and attitudes
to sustain the world
and human civilization
with humility and humanity.

Let's not live with a false belief
and sense of security that
the New year will change
everything for better.
The line that exists
between the two years

is like an invisible line
drawn on ocean water.

The year two thousand twenty was
only a cog in the wheel of infinite Time
and is now wedged into the
heart of two thousand twenty one,
like a painful, revengeful nail
shedding blood for ever.

Death is Marching

Death is smashing many a lock
with his horrible heartless hammer,
to steal many of my friends' fortune
like an invincible ruthless robber.

Daily I hear the pounding of
Death's mallet on someone's door,
treasures are snatched away with temerity
as Death puts people into terrible torture.

Human life is now transformed into
a formidable bane with no light of respite,
men and women are manacled by Corona
omnipotent Death is marching into every street.

The poignant procession of dead humans
seems to be unbearably unending,
the loud noise of knell is heard everywhere
as dreadful Death's horrendous wagon comes galloping.

Supreme Power

Tiger ! Tiger, are you listening ?
Are you awake or leisurely sleeping ??

Are you aware of that tiny thing,
Which has become so very terrifying
By tightening its grip on human beings ?

Your position as the unchallenged king
amongst animals, is its importance losing.
An unheard of power is spreading its wings,
Men in millions she is ruthlessly killing.

Tiger Tiger, are you hearing ?
Or, are you afraid like men and hibernating ?
Hearken to the lethal foot steps thumping,
The world is filled with fears resounding.
Coronation of Corona as supreme
queen is fortifying.

(Composed on International Tiger's Day)

Mahalaxmi: Emancipation Incarnated

You are the goddess
of wealth and good fortune,
revered and worshipped as the
consort of Lord Jagannath,
adored for your ideal of equality
that cuts across the age old
barrier of caste system.
Your blessings shower like
rain water on pious souls
like Shreeya the untouchable woman
while shunning rich upper caste
but unclen households.

The myth surrounding your
imperial personality makes you
a champion of women's empowerment.
Through your characterization
is told a centuries old tale of
subversive women who rose
above the traditional feminine roles,
challenging male domination
while not forgetting to carry out
their duties and responsibilities.

Your emergence as an emancipated
woman, questioning the verdict
of your husband and disapproval
of his elder brother Balabhadra,
flashes like a thunderbolt
in their Autumnal sky of life.

No feminist of this twenty first century
can match your powerful sense
of self esteem as you leave
the house of God, the temple
of Lord Jagannath removing all your
precious ornaments rejecting the Lord's plea.
You leave not the temple like a
docile helpless woman shedding
silent tears and seeking the help of parents.

You swear in the name of Supernatural powers
to prove your purity and impartiality
and your soulful imprecations transform
the life of Lord Jagannath and Balabhadra
into a series of pitiable afflictions.
The temple turns into a doomed
deserted place and the Lords are driven
from pillar to post for a morsel of food.
At your behest goddess Saraswati
and gods like Varuna, Surya and Agni
become hostile to them.

Tired and hungry at last they come begging
for food to your palatial house built by Viswakarma.
Your victory is complete with the Lord's
final submission, acquitting you of
all charges and accepting your demands.

You stand unique as a symbol
of balanced womanhood.

True Contentment

Happiness is a cherished goal of life,
To acquire it man's endeavor is unending;
But bliss is not a commodity easily bought,
It's a feeling experienced with heavenly blessings.

Mortal man measures the pleasures of life,
With money, wealth and worldly assets;
Money is mercurial and wealth has wings,
Which quite often the foolish being forgets.

Running madly to enjoy more earthly ecstasy,
Man cares not for virtuous things;
Love, sympathy and peace are neglected,
Life is wasted and lived with only suffering.

Deceive not yourself with decomposed ideas,
Look within and learn to love and give;
Train the mind to drink like a swan,
And swim calmly on all turbulent tides.

True contentment is savoured by gaining virtues,
And leading a selfless dedicated life;
May all human beings remember this always,
To make life meaningful and stop all strife.

Moments to Remember

A strange farewell was that.

No dew drops glistened on
the shining star of eyes.
No thumping sounded in
the heart with apprehensions
of losing a treasure.

That was the pinnacle of
waiting for many long days;
waiting with silent love and
doubt and petulance and sometimes
bitter quarrels over petty things.
All that ended at
that moment of parting.
The lips that had not
dared to open the gates
of heart, trembled.
A pleasant pain -
Two pairs of eyes devoured
and savoured each other.
Still the lips did not
utter the words.

We knew words were superfluous.

A few moments of parting
while we forgot everything else
and were united in the
most intimate terms without
even touching each other.

The moments passed,
we burst into hilarious laughter,
while people stared at us
with disbelief.

Be a Winged Woman

Freedom is not to be acquired as alms,
Power should not be procured with penitence
Unchained you were born and
unfettered you must live.
Break open all the burdensome shackles
that are encircling your hands and feet,
your mind, thoughts and actions.

Take wings now !
Mustering all courage and strength
soar high into the sky like a
seagull over the vast ocean of life.
You are a magnificent creation of God
born beautiful with versatile talents
to achieve glory reaching greater heights.

When life compels you to savour
unlimited sufferings with unpleasant
disparity and unbearable injustices
never allow these unwanted negative things
to take over your marvelous skill.
Learn the art of draining these out of life
like a seagull flushing out
excess salt from saline water.

Flap your wings and rise above the dismal life,
Glide with grace to accomplish your distant dream.

The Wander-Lust Lover

The aroma of Spring is wafting in the air
and deadly chilly Winter days are gone;
The meadows are aflame with iridescent flowers
birds are singing on trees with sweet tone.

The fragrance of love is spreading like fire
men and women are frolicking recklessly on shore ;
Preys of passion, they must be planning
a grand Valentines celebration with fun galore.

Where are you darling, my long lost lover
in which country are you staying now ?
My heart pines for your presence by my side
but you seem to have forgotten the sacred vow.

Come back home flying like migratory birds,
test not my patience like a hard taskmaster;
A few months of your company can rejuvenate me,
to distant lands then you are free to wander.

In My Prayers

You were in my prayers
all these days when an
impish storm was raging
and you were thrown unawares
into the inferno of a dark
dangerous forest by a tornado.

Like Prometheus defying Divinity,
challenging the norms of society,
even refusing to accept sanity,
you were roaming directionless,
like a maniac in search of your
Aphrodite, real or imaginary.

Heedless of consequences,
careless about the deadly snakes
coiled around each unsuspecting tree;
you got lost in the labyrinthine lanes
of a lugubrious dreamland, when
your spurious admirers followed you
with daggers in hand to back stab you
and furious fires encircled you.

For days and nights
the thunderstorm continued,
deafening, crackling sounds followed
as the cosmos seemed torn apart.

Lightenings flashed repeatedly
across the firmament
blinding the eyes.

Fearlessly you stood
inviting the celestial current
to pass through your mortal frame;
to cleanse you, forge you and
mould you on the anvil of Love.

I remained still
with bated breath
and stifled heart
chanting prayers for you.

Like a Phoenix you rose
out of your ashes and
I stretched out my trembling
arms, to hide you inside the coil
of a sacred, secret conch shell.

In my prayers
you always remain,
for I adore you and
care for you like a Meera
worshipping her Krishna.

Soliloquy of December Flower

Like royal glamorous ladies
we flowers are fashionable
and forget not to flaunt our
splendour with pulchritude.

Sophisticated names are desired
even by small diminutive flowers.
A name that can spell charisma,
can allure a spectator with
hypnotic power.

How dull and dreary it is
to call me with a prosaic name
like December Flower !!
The month of my annual birth
tagged to a nondescript, common
word like flower !

Scientists are more artistic than you.
They call me with a romantic name
Barleria Cristata, but you my admirers
seem to be swept away by
my rival flowers.

Like a blue-blooded beautiful dame
my petals are violet in colour,
Some people call me "Philippines Violet"
and if you don't like that nomenclature
please call me in my other sweeter name
"Bluebell Barleria", but for Heaven's sake
never call me as December Flower.

Rain In March

Heralding dangerous dark clouds,
unexpectedly after a white-hot day
In the afternoon of first or second
week of sweltering March,
every year comes Poseidon
galloping on his angry horse
and suddenly the earth is
shrouded with a black blanket
of Hellish mystery.

The trident of Poseidon tears apart
the sky with thousand holes and
torrential rain comes tumbling down
on the earth, accompanied by
jasmine like hailstones.

Thunder-clouds blaze with
Indra's iridescent weaponry.
Innocents working on farm lands,
busy with the task of providing
food for humanity, are struck
dead by thunderbolt.

But today was a
differently pleasant day.
Rain drizzled in the evening
for the first time after a calm

cloudy day filled with
soft glowing sunlight.

The drops of rain fell slowly
on my balcony, and my roof-top,
on houses, lanes and trees with
graceful rhythm of a ballet dancer.
And the aroma of wet soil conquered
over the fragrance of flowers.

It seemed as if Nature had
become matured like me
with no boisterous laughter,
no tempestuous feelings and
no schizophrenic outbursts.
Only a calm, serene blissful mind
reposed in the lap of Nature.

Enigmatic Eyes

Haunted was I
by a pair of enigmatic eyes.
Eyes so mysterious and baffling,
miraculous and mystifying.
The glance powerful and penetrating,
eternally engrossed in X-raying.
Their charisma, a strange synthesis
of repulsion and attraction.

Like the eyes of a Tantric,
worshipper of some occult cult,
their silent speech closely cryptic.

I dared not meet them point-blank.
Their gaze seemed to maze me,
encircling like a python too suffocating.

Avoidance was a temporary solution.
Escape futile magnified into
a magical, magnetic fascination.

Strange that the haunting eyes
were in reality haunted eyes.
The agonized petals desperate
to hide hurts and wounds
sufferings and frustrations.

Stealthily I tried to fathom
the unfathomable sea;
to uncode the cryptography
of their recondite resonance.
But impossible was to split
the truth, through prism
of these eyes into different
hues of human mind.

Leave them or love them !!
Came a command from above.
My subconscious self preferred to love.

Within a few seconds
the inscrutable became crystalline;
The arcane words sounded like
a sweet savoury language,
the terrifying look transformed
into cherubic childishness.
And my trepidations turned
into pleasant palpitations.

A Game of Chess

Two poets
were engrossed in a
friendly game of chess,
using words and phrases
as king, queen and knights,
rooks, bishops and pawns.

The unwritten cardinal codes
of the game were accepted
by both in silence.

No one was
to be the winner.
Each time after checkmate
one poet recited a poem
using words mostly of one colour.

Then the table
was turned.
Game continued
until the other poet
composed another poem
using words consequential
stolen from the first poem.

Open stealing was enjoyed
by both the poets

sitting face to face
with rarely meeting eyes,
their hearts and minds
concentrated on
each step to be taken
in this brainstorming game.

Ignorant spectators
unaware of the parameters
controlling this aesthetic play
frowned with puzzlement.
Gullible visitors tried to guess
the meaning of this strange game
gazing into it with
their jaundiced eyes.

All of a sudden, one day
the cosmos reverberated
with a malignant rumour.
To the amused amazement
of the poet players
this game of chess was
branded as a game of
improper amour.

Heartless hounders
ambushed the poets.
The game of chess ended.

But the two ingenious poets
continued to just live and breathe
their poetry profound,
Leaving the ambuscadoes
crestfallen and pondering
again how to hound.

Strange Meeting

Strange that you came to meet me
After building such chasms wide,
You came with all your passionate love
And stood with burning desire by my side.

You seemed to be possessed by
An evil spirit, bent upon casting
Your satanic spell on my honest heart
Around my waist your hands were encircling.

But I had no feelings for you
I didn't enjoy your embrace,
With disapproving eyes I disentangled
Your hands, saving me from disgrace.

My displeasure at your proximity
Couldn't hinder you from claiming me openly,
Again you tried to encircle your tentacles
With an insane intention, as I shivered bitterly.

It was a meaningless meeting
For our love is long lost and dead,
Strange that you came in my dream
Gifting callousness to my heart and head.

Worth of A Woman

To judge the purity of a woman's soul
if you ask the life-giving evanescent Air;
Carrying a whiff of fragrance from flowery garden
Air would tell how her soul is fresh and fair.

To measure the breadth of a woman's heart
if you seek the opinion of azure expansive Sky;
Sky will look down silently with humility
at her genial heart feeling utterly shy.

To fathom the depth of a woman's mind
if you request for the view of saline Sea;
Sea waves would nod their heads with ignorance
like a child playing nonchalantly on life's lea.

To assess the power of a woman's body
if you plead before the evergreen Earth;
Tears would roll down from Earth's eyes with
sympathy for her untold endurance and strength.

Never try to estimate the worth of a woman
for she is a replica of the Supreme Creator;
Soothing cool moonbeams fall from her eyes
and the Sun shines on her forehead as sindoor.

Invocation to Maa Ambika

The Autumnal sky is threading a silvery garland
of little rambling clouds silky and soft;
The rain-washed fresh air is slowly humming
sweet euphoric Invocation songs oft.

The Earth is delicately decorating herself
with myriad flowers of various hue;
Your devoted children are eagerly waiting
for the holy celebration and to welcome you.

O' Mahisasurmardini Maa !!
Descend from your heavenly abode
to glorify the Earth and bless your devotees;
The world is ravaged by Mahisha in different shapes,
kill them all with your invincible trident
making them numb with your omnipotent eyes.

Appear as Annada in Paddy fields
Let there be no desolate deaths due to hunger;
As Debanshi Devi Durga smite all evils
with merciless determination and gifted power.

You are also Uma and Adi Parashakti,
as Rudrakali you partake in Tandav of Shiva;
to protect the helpless innocents
and punish the unholy miscreants.

Before the unchallenged
reigns of all Mahishas
turn this blessed earth into a hell,
arrive with your army of pious progenies
loudly ringing these demons' death knell.

Momentary

Ah ! What's this dreadful voice
Haunting me - nearer and nearer,
Like the scream of a monster ?

Where am I going?
Where is my harbour ?
To which place the water
Of this river is flowing ??

Where is the boatman !
Why my oars are hanging vainly
Against the sharp flowing water ?

My stern is broken
My seam is becoming wider and wider,
The keel-nail has loosened the garboard.

Here is chilly darkness all around.
The cool breeze is growing violent,
But alas ! No one is with me.

What has happened to all ?
Ah, who will help me now ?
Lest I merge in river.

Yet that voice I hear,
Indistinct, enigmatic.
That voice, that voice -
A roar, a dirge
A mixture, a confusion.

Let's Take a Solemn Pledge

Let's take a solemn pledge of
allegiance to this firmamental globe,
to our greater homeland
lying desolate due to our negligence.
Let's make it beautiful again.

Let's plant as many trees as we can
and rear them like our own children
who in return would give us more oxygen.
Let's swear by the name of Mother Earth
to stop deforestation and forest fire
by vested interests operating
like cruel, callous monsters.

Let's keep clean and uncontaminated
all the springs and rivers
which run on this wonderful planet
like arteries and veins in human body,
sustaing all the living organisms.
Let's make a promise to keep
our environment clean and comfortable
to make it a pollution free healthy place
for all to live in peace.

Let's reduce our wants by cutting
down our unnecessary purchases
which at the end turn into garbages.

Let's cultivate an attitude to reuse things
as long as it can be made useful
in some form or other.
Let's not add mindlessly more things
to the stinking dumping yards
by throwing away our own
'use and throw' mentality.

Let's learn all the lessons
that the present pandemic has
taught us in last few months.
Let's remember that the Earth is not
only for us, the human beings.
Let's not forget our duties and
responsibilities towards other things.
Let's show humility in our behavior
and charity in our treatment
of other living beings.
Their lives are as valuable as ours.

Let's take a Divine pledge
to protect this Earth, or else
one day, the Earth may devour us.

From Lamborghini to Chemborghini

Natural calamity like Death
is the best leveller,
in putting rich and poor
on the same rostrum.
Nature makes no distinction
on the basis of material possessions
when she pours her blessings
or wrecks with vengeance
the world of puny creatures
like we human beings.

Proud and rich mother
of two illustrious sons
shining like stars in the
Malayalam tinsel world;
You had a grudge against
the narrow street that
led to your house.
You had pressed upon
the Public Works Department to
get the road repaired for your
new sedan Lamborghini.
Before the government could
comply to your complaint,
Nature gave an answer.

And you had to be rescued
not on luxurious wheels
but in an aluminum vessel
through the flooded narrow lane.

Yours is an instance
of man's insignificance and
all his bravado's unimportance.

Man's insidious attempts
to put Nature under control
turning insipid and his insolence
making him incapacitated.
He cringes with fear and gapes at
the inconceivable power of Nature,
with awe, being crippled in mind and body,
benumbed by the beaconic blow of Nature,
frazzled by the fury of wounded Nature.

This is a lesson to be learnt by all,
to learn to live in harmony with Nature.
And to lead life with humility and
thankfulness to the great Creator.

Another Philomela

I revered you as my God,
never suspected your real intention
hidden behind the soothing sweet words
and your play acting as a trickster.

Enticed by the charm of
your endearing words of encomium,
I innocently allowed myself
to be carried away with the
current of your vengeful designs.
You took pleasure in ravishing me publicly
with naked descriptions of my physique.
From my toes to my hairs, inch by inch,
you portrayed me in your poems
with voluptuous words aimed at
arousing longing and erotic feelings.

It was worse than a physical rape.
I felt like an object for auction.
My sacred body laid bare in market place
for everybody to see, examine
and enjoy a vicarious pleasure.

What was my crime ?
Why did you make me a scapegoat
of your bitterness for the rejection
you suffered as a jilted lover ??

Fearing the revelation of truth
you silenced me permanently.
I couldn't explain to the world
the heartbreaking truth lying
under an apparent mystery.
And the veracity of my personality
was buried in the dark hollow of history.

Power of Camouflaging

In the country of Futile Fame,
In the forest of Passion Fire,
Continued the hounding of a small hare.

Ignorant was she
of the intention of Hounders,
Immersed she remained
in her little homely pleasures;
illuminating her inconspicuous life
with inspirations from invisible God.

Never did the hare dare to
incite the animals of prey,
but hounders are after all
by nature always predators.
They feel themselves as impotent
if they fail to kill an innocent.

Chased by the Cheetahs and Lions
Pestered by the Panthers and Tigers
Harassed by the Hyenas and Wolves
Fervently prayed the hare for her safety.
God listened to her ardent entreaty
and gave a boon to hare petite.

Insubstantial was she
in the eyes of predators,

Iridescent became she
with power of camouflaging,
transforming herself
into a tortoise,
living an amphibious life
at her own sweet will.

A Mother: Not Mother-in-Law

I don't know why
but each time I think
about you, a big lump
chokes my throat and
my eyes get flooded with tears.
There are even times when
my usual dry eyes know
no bounds and an uncontrollable
sob wells up blinding me and
shaking my whole being.

You were the only solace,
my pillar of support in
my battered life devastated
by misfortunes.
Your company was enough
to wipe away all my disgruntled
feelings caused by misunderstanding
and callousness of others.

Many a times I reminisce
the days we spent together
in the village home, silent
like an ascetic's cottage.
Unforgettable are those
evening hours with usual
power cuts and a dim lantern

burning in the verandah.
You sitting by my side would be
narrating many of your old vignettes;
sometimes revealing your age-old
expertise in curing people with
traditional medicine prepared
from leaves and flowers and roots.
Alas !! Now I wish I should have
noted down that knowledge from you.

Wide gap of age between us
had never been a barrier in our
perfect understanding of each other.
Rather quite often I felt as if
you were my long lost grand mother
with whom I could be as free and happy
as a little girl with an angel.
In spite of all my failings
you were never cross with me.
Rather I felt as if your heart was
all the time praying for my wellbeing.

So far I have not seen another woman
so positive and soothing like you,
like a moon-lit night pouring blessings.
You were as strong as a mountain
and as broad minded as a vast ocean.
And probably for this you could live
up to the ripe old age of hundred and six,
fighting the battle of a widowed life
for fifty six years, raising six children
amidst many adverse times.

Give me a chance Bou,
to be born as your daughter
in my next birth, so that
I can repay you what I owe to you
and do whatever I couldn't do
in this birth because of circumstances
and also learn from you, how to
lead a successful century old life.

A Victim of Fani

You had bridged too wide a time gap
of more than two and half millenniums,
from the time of prince Gautam till today.
You had attained salvation from mere tree life
with the enlightenment of Lord Buddha.
Like a Buddhist monk you had traversed
from India to Sri Lanka on a holy mission.
With the pious love of daughter Sanghamitra
of king Ashoka, you grew in Anuradhapur
and from there you came to Bhubaneswar
in the balmy hands of a Burmese Prime Minister.

You grew with grace and glory
like the original sacred Bodhi tree,
standing stubbornly for sixty six years
in the beautiful precincts of Buddha mandir,
Your leafy canopy sheltering hundred
and eight golden Buddha statues, spreading
the doctrine of detachment and non-violence.

Bathed in myriad memories of Buddhist culture
and history, the ancient temple city of
Bhubaneswar had cradled you unharmed
even during the Super cyclone that had
rammed and ravaged her twenty years ago.
But she failed to protect you from
the fatal blows of Fani which licked her
like a thousand headed hydra.

You fell down like a defenceless child
bowing down before the brutal blows
of a benevolent Mother Nature, who had
suddenly turned malevolent due to
some unfathomable reasons, making
all completely vulnerable.

(Poem composed on the sacred Boddhi tree of Bhubaneswar that was uprooted by cyclone Fani in March 2019. The Prime Minister of Burma, Yu Nu had brought a sapling from Anuradhapur and planted it on 13th May 1953.)

A Dream Not Fulfilled

Sitting around the breakfast table
we were engrossed in animated talks,
like a coterie of studious children
bubbling with ideas of a discovery.
Our minds filled with visions of
birthplace of ShriRam, Hanumangarhi
and other religious sites in Ayodhya
were desperate to solve the mystery.
Our unplanned visit to an ancient land
and holy river Sarayu to be
a part of our history.

The cynosure of everyone was
the spectacular and captivating model
of proposed Ram Temple to be built on
the exact place, believed by millions of
Hindus to be the birthplace of ShriRam.
That was the year of Nineteen ninety
and we were a group of college teachers
from different parts of India.
A classless Sunday had thrown
an opportunity to us to visit
Ayodhya and quench our thirst
for reaching the truth
behind Babri Masjid.

The truth is still a mystery for many.
The debate is rumbling on the road
of uncertainty even after three decades,
while a cherished dream remains unfulfilled,
locked in the cupboards of law and order.

As I ruminate now on
my feelings of that day,
the voice of a Parsi friend
comes floating through memory lanes
like an undaunted spirit of hope amidst
the present gloomy lugubrious scenarios.

He had laughed at me
for leading our group from
Lucknow to Ayodhya simply
to satisfy my inquisitive mind.
But with strong conviction had added
"If innumerable Hindus believe that
Rama was born at that place, then
that is the truth, for in religion
truth is nothing but belief".

Autumnal Full Moon

Patiently like an angler I stood
to catch a glimpse of the full moon
in an overcast Autumnal sky.

Like a lass suffering from lassitude
under constant harassment
from maniacal men,
the moon preferred to hide
her face behind the dark clouds.
When my hope was submerged in uncertainties,
suddenly the moon removed her cloudy veil
presenting to me a lachrymose look.
The poor moonlight poured out her
tears betraying her helplessness in
protecting the young girls
who worship her annually to be blessed
with a loving handsome husband.

Ignorant are these innocent girls about
the inhuman intention of human panthers
who have discarded Pantheism
in their insane carnal desire and
have turned into devilish murderers.

The moon goddess simply stands
as a silent witness to their torture.

Fisherman's Wife

My man goes out to sea in a small boat
when from east spreads a streak of silver;
With the waves his boat dances dangerously
and then sails smoothly on distant water.

With rippling waves touching my feet, I watch
the boat becoming a dot in faraway horizon;
I retrace my reluctant steps slowly homeward
as sky gets splashed with radiant colours of sun.

I pray the Sea God to protect my man
and thank him for giving us a livelihood;
To Sun and Sand I offer my thankfulness
for fostering our love from our childhood.

My man is my best friend and guide
deep as the sea is our mutual love;
When he returns with boat full of fishes
we prefer to sit at home like a pair of dove.

My Neighbour's Pride

Owner's pride is
neighbour's pleasure.

No !! Don't say
that I am wrong.
That it is a misquotation
of the popular Tv ad.
That it is envy not pleasure.

Envy is like
a wreath of Olives
worn around the forehead
by winners of ancient Olympics.

I am not a winner.
Nor do I want to
join any race of
fame and fortune
of love and luxury.

Happy am I amidst
all sorts of misery.
In a life of deprivation
and degradation,
for my invincible spirit is
beyond the power of destruction.

I like to wear
a tiara of Lavender,
to be blessed with
peace and tranquillity.
Pure rapture is my reward
when Happiness puts
his indelible signature
in the house of my neighbour
terminating their midnight
quarrels in entirety.

Where Are You Anamika

Where are you Anamika !!
Where are you after
forty-one years of our first meeting !
Whose heart are you girdling now
with your ocean deep eyes ?
Where have you built your
lovely nest that was denied
to you in your childhood ?

Your face flashed before my eyes today
suddenly after I saw a photograph,
the eyes of which cascaded all
my pleasant memories of you,
breaking open the floodgates of time.
Something pricked at my heart
and my soulful longing to see you
again started brimming with
the sorrowful cup of my life.

A vision stood still in which
I saw you for the first time.
A tearful whimpering little being,
a three years old tiny tinsel doll
clutching at the hands of her
grandmother, looking helplessly
into the eyes of her elder sister;
refusing and resisting with

all her futile might to go
to the nursery class; while the
grandmother was enumerating
in hushed tones to the Principal
how you two daughters were dumped
by your father, an Army officer,
after your mother committed suicide.

You had burst into pitiable loud cries,
after your heartbroken grandparents
went away forcibly leaving you
with the care of teachers.
You had tugged my saree, clasping
my legs for comfort and consolation.
And as I lifted you up in my arms,
patting your shoulders
your sobbing had suddenly stopped.
I don't know what you saw in me but
each day you would run towards me
in the morning assembly and
would hold me tight refusing to go
to your class with your teacher.

While your elder sister had suddenly
grown up into a mature girl after
the personal shock, you
remained a crying baby,
posing a lot of trouble for
the teachers in your school.
Among all the chattering, laughing,
crying and fighting little angels
of nursery class,
you were a dumb doll,

shedding tears like a
perennial waterfall and the
only answer that you used to give
for all questions and queries was
your name Anamika.... Anamika.....

Though sobered a little after one month
of schooling, no teacher was able
to keep you inside the class;
for very stealthily almost mysteriously
you would run away and come to
the class where I would be teaching
and would sit silently on a little box
that was kept in the corner
and would continue to stare at me.

Many a times I was held responsible
for your wayward behaviour and had
to warn you, though lovingly but
the result would be your heart rending cry
that used to shut up all complaining mouths.

Much water has flown in the river Mahanadi
and Time has travelled forty-one years.
But O' dear Anamika, my sweet Anamika,
the picture of your little innocent sad face
with talkative eyes, is imprinted in
my mind's canvas with indelible ink.

A Silver Medal

Run Dutee, run
to win more medals
for India and to shine
like the auspicious, silvery
full moon of today.
Run to make India as well as
Odisha proud of you.
Run to prove your mettle
and to silence your critics.
To show everyone
what a determined woman
can do amidst deterring situations.

The temporary ban
imposed on you
couldn't put any shackles
on your galloping feet.
Neither the questioning eyes
douse your burning spirit.

Run on the track of life.
Jump over the hurdles of life.
For LIFE rewards those
who know how to take
the challenges of life,
turning each one of these
apparently insurmountable obstacles
into silver or gold medals.

Friendship for Me

Friendship is like the glowing
morning sunlight adding warmth
and inspiration to the waning year,
An energy booster, bringing light of hope
in moments of frustration filled tears.

Friendship is like flowers blooming
in the night, filling life with its
sweet memorable fragrance,
Silently and slowly it permeates
one's personality, paving the path of life
with loving remembrance.

Friendship is like the gentle murmuring
brook, listening to all our feelings
with a sympathetic song.
A true blessing in the tormented life
giving comfort when anything goes wrong.

Friendship is like the flashing
glimmering ripples of water in a pond,
when a stone is thrown,
A note that touches every string of heart
creating caring music when
a melancholic wind is blown.

Friendship is like the pearly drop of water
on blades of grass at dusky dawn,
A dainty, delicate, dazzling feeling
that should never be used as pawn.

May Peace Prevail

May my words be inadequate to offer
Gratitude to the benevolent God
For saving us from the wrath
Of turbulent hostile Nature.

May my heart hang down with shame
And repentance for the wavering faith
In the Supreme Creator and
The miraculous power of soulful prayers.

May I and the Humanity never stop
From learning the timely teachings
Of our heavenly father, imparted to us
In innumerable indirect ways.

May peace prevail everywhere
May a deep calmness overpower
The human mind and actions,
The Universe and the Earth,
The Nature and all living beings.

May there be complete order and serenity
With harmony, concord and tranquility.

Music of Monitor

Wake up, wake
Wake up, wake up.
Incessantly sings the monitor
not taking a single break.

The patient sleeps on,
apathetic to the warning call.

Pulse rate slow,
Oxygen level sometimes normal,
Blood pressure fluctuating like
the mood of a quarrelsome husband,
The graph of heartbeat serrated like
the toddler's first attempt at drawing.

Beep, beep
Sleep, sleep
sings the monitor
sarcastically.

Sleep runs away like
a truant child from the door
of healthy person's anxious eyes
lying miserably on attendant's bed.
The solemn tune of monitor
slowly gets mixed up with the
distant ringing of death knell.

To my Friend Baruna

Dear Baruna !
To ask you any questions I have no right,
for I had failed to infuse the requisite might;
in our friendship that could have helped
to dispel the darkness in which you groped
before deciding to draw the black curtain
in the drama of your life.

What's that dark destructive force
which caught hold of your beautiful brain
like tenacious tentacles dragging you to death ?
How could you leave so unexpectedly
just a fortnight before your birthday ?
What mysterious attractions of Death
enticed you so much that you preferred to
bid farewell to your family and friends ??
Why did you lock your feelings inside
your heart so ruthlessly that it
stole away your lovable life ??

Why....why Oh why
my dear childhood friend
why and how could you do this ?
Your desperate act seems to have
wiped out one colour after another
from the rainbow filled days
of people who loved you,

How could you forget that no one
could bear a death of such hue ??
My heart was bleeding profusely
by being the helpless spectator
of a long procession of known people
leaving one after the other:
But the news of your death came
like a bolt from the blue making me
numb, dumb and bitter.
Too much was its powerful blow,
I fail to reconcile myself
to the painful truth till now.

As I think of you Baruna,
the face that floats before my eyes
is that of an innocent school girl
bubbling with mirth and
my tears refuse to obey
my grown-up mind;
I try to find an answer
to all my questions
but no one responds and
no solution do I find.

And the jest for life is lost
in the wilderness of uncertainty;
Life and death are juxtaposed
I find only suffering in my vicinity.

A Victim's Last Word

Don't ask me how I am feeling
For now I neither feel nor think nor cry;
I am a victim of the worst crime
Yet I have no self-pity nor I feel shy.

They forgot that I am a living human being
Treated me as an object for their carnal pleasure;
They gagged me and tied my hands with rope
Like deadly demons they destroyed my virgin treasure.

They threw me disdainfully in the dry drain
Like a dog throwing away the leg piece mutton;
They assumed that I had lost my life, but
My spirit fought bravely their physical glutton.

For last fifteen days my body is fighting
Hopelessly for life on this hospital bed
My name has become a news headline
I hate to hear this and soon I'll be dead.

Drag those ogres out of the dark dungeons
Where they are hiding and fulfil my last wish;
Let them stand stark naked in a crowded square
Tied to lamp posts, wriggling like a netted fish.

Play of Chromosomes

Time has changed only artificially.
So to say, just ornamentally.
Fact remains as it was
many centuries ago.

Time is still standing still.

A chauvinistic father debars his
daughter from pursuing higher studies;
And sells his family estate in
a bout of drunkenness.
Years after the same daughter
saves her family honour,
buys back the parental property
with her hard earned money.

Sudden brain stroke.
A father is paralyzed
No ambulance.
A daughter drives in midnight
to admit her father in hospital.

A tragedy in life makes
a father incapable.
The eldest daughter nullifies
her own prospective marriage,
dedicates her whole life for
the bright future of six siblings.

Father serious
Mother not well.
A daughter comes
rushing from Canada
to be with parents,
leaving behind her own
husband, children and
professional obligations.

Father is bedridden,
unable to hold a pen.
A daughter sacrifices
her own pleasures and
sits by his bed, for long hours.
Meticulously she notes down
all the poems and stories
dictated by her writer father.

Father leaves behind
an intellectual empire.
Most likely to be rusted
without proper care.
A daughter comes forward
to fulfil her father's dream,
at the cost of her own comforts.

A father is murdered.
Daughter takes a silent vow
to take revenge on conspirators.
Risking her own life, she
befriends the enemy camp.

Oh ! So many cases are there.
So much is done by the daughters
for their fathers - their childhood hero.
But why can't some fathers realize
the true worth of diamond like daughters !

Killed in the womb,
suffocated after birth
thrown in the gutters,
discarded in orphanages or
exchanged with another's son.
Suffering of survivors is no less.

Perpetrators of such crimes
are the biological fathers.
Why are these fathers
so averse to daughters !!
Why do they remain perpetually
angry with their wives for
not begetting a son !
Why do they fail to understand
that birth is only a coincidental play
of male and female chromosomes !!

To My Mother

You are now a
picture framed beautifully,
put on a pedestal and
worshipped annually
only to be forgotten
for rest of the days.

Artistically decorated with
garlands of colourful flowers,
you look graceful and gorgeous,
a brass lamp burns luminous,
aroma from incense sticks
float in the whole house.
You seem to be satisfied
with contentment oozing out
from each corner of our home.

But is it the reality ??

All the pomp and ceremony
of your remembrance day
hides the harrowing truth
of your real life imprisoned
inside the boundary wall of a
half century old two storied house.

A deafening silence
sits in each room
alternatively with
loud clang from
sneaking suspicion
and blatant accusations.

Your framed photo
trembles with fear;
Apprehensions of a
future devastation
fill your eyes with tears.

I am one of your
worthless progenies,
that's why you refused
to recognize me today and
Papa turned his face away
from me when I went
to my childhood home
in the dream
of dawn.

My Laments

When a hobby
becomes a passion;
when the passion
turns into an obsession,
probably a door is opened
for an uninvited guest
called Destruction
to disturb your blissful
land of oblivion
by making a
dangerous intrusion.

My love for photography
has landed me now in
a state of constant troubles
and my mind is filled with
remorse and repentance.

Without my knowledge
all my beautiful and memorable
pictures are wiped out
of my phone gallery
one after the other
quite mysteriously like
a magician's sleight of wand
or witchcraft of an evil soul.

Come as My Bridegroom

Inevitable is your
arrival in my life,
but inscrutable are
your ways and intentions.

Daily I can hear
the muffled sound of your forceful
footsteps, secretively
approaching my mortal mansion.

Kindly don't knock on
my unexpected door
when I am completely unprepared
to welcome you O' Death !!

Please give me at least
a few days' notice
to deck myself up
properly as a willing bride
and bid a fortuitous farewell
to my dear ones.

Come as my boisterous bridegroom
to claim me, to carry me away
to your land of Eternal Rest
on the sacred palanquin of
six pieces of bamboo.

Merry in May

When the scorching Sun starts
pouring molten lava on Earth;
when the Air turns awful and
uninviting for frolicksome flowers
of cold, cosy winter months;

When the mighty terrible Summer
embarks upon his annual journey
on desolate depressed Earth,
the Easter Lilies awaken from sleep
and raise their long straight shoulders.

With big bold petals painted with
passionate pigments, these Lilies smile
and dance merrily in April and May,
nodding their heads with gratefulness
singing the song of perseverance.

A Chiselled Marvel

Ensconced on a small pedestal
you are sitting inside a gallery in
Philadelphia Museum of Arts flag;
proudly displaying before inquisitive visitors
the magnificence of Indian artistry,
a symbol of defiance against Time's drag.

Imprisoned for years inside a
glass house, you seem to be
brooding over the bygone Era,
the time of your incredible creation
and the long labyrinthine journey you
were forced to take from India to America.

Which craftsman's dexterous fingers
did the intricate carvings on your
delicate body, transforming a simple
conch shell into an exquisite piece of art
to be treasured and safeguarded as holy
Sankh in a temple to hold the sacred water?

Who is that first insolent infidel who dared to
steal you and sell you for a handful of rupees ?
What is the name of that art connoisseur
who salvaged you from the heinous hands
of international smugglers, gauging your
great value as an astonishing antique piece ??

Beyond the boundaries of geography and
Time, you sit with calm silence like Buddha,
meditating on the transience of human life
and immortality of transcendental art.

Perennially blessed by God Vishnu whose
image is aesthetically carved on your
tusk like stout body along with Garuda,
you tell the tale of ancient Indian culture.
Adorned in the upper panel by the image of
elephant headed Ganesh and many more,
you seem to be summoning all with
a mute but measured message.
Sanctified and strengthened by ageless
glory, you beckon the passers-by with
an open invitation to watch you keenly and
feel the fragrance of a phenomenal country.

Your undesirable rigorous travel
was probably predestined by Vishnu
with a purpose to emanate Indian culture.

(This poem is inspired by the picture of a conch shell posted by a Facebook site named "Worldwide Hindu Temples".)

No More

No more
do I wait
for a heart warming
Good night message.
No more do I
remain awake till
late hours in night
to read your soothing,
consoling words, framed
beautifully inside
your digital art.

There was a time
when your nights
didn't start without
my goodnight text.
Daily you would wait,
your hunger not satiated
till you savoured those
saccharined sweets, which
as you used to say made
you feel cared for.

Bitterly sweet
Sweetly sour
Pleasantly sorrowful
was our relationship.

Indelible incidents
Memorable moments
Unforgettable feelings
pile up in the locked
cupboard of my heart.
Mind refuses to abide
by the advice of
intellect or reason.

I have no regrets
no acrimony
nor any complaints.

From the beginning
we had taken the journey
without a trace of seriousness,
like two strange passengers
in a train, trying to make
the few hours of togetherness
pleasant and memorable.

Your memory will
always touch my heart
like sea waves touching
the shore making me
happy and contented.

Masquerade

Mysterious arts of camouflaging
is practiced and perfected by human beings
both in real life and social media,
learning it with impunity from flora and fauna.
Mind boggling masks are worn well
for days after days, even years after years
with immaculate offensive illusory wiles,
like the angler fish or octopus.
Like chameleons, constant change of
colour is modulated by mortal mankind
but rarely for protective purposes
to sustain in the struggling life.

Life is turned into a perennial masquerade
and one is perpetually perturbed about
the real identity of the person walking beside.
A golden gossamer is ceaselessly spun
by the veiled visages with their eyes
searching for possible preys.
These cobwebs move like roulette wheels
and the unfortunate innocent victim
falls like a betting ball into their desired slot.

Ravana had ten faces but
all were similar and Hitler
is said to have kept many look-alikes
to protect himself from enemies.

But today's masked men
have innumerable inconsistent countenances
of masculine or feminine, flora or fauna,
mundane or terrestrial facade.

Like a mystery play it is interesting to watch
but impossible to unravel the enigma
or solve the riddle lying behind.
The puzzle is permanent,
for the visor is often vicious
with mastered maneuvers.

My Tears

Happiness at
an exceptional discovery
about self, now flows
profusely with tears.

A deep pang
goes on stabbing
my heart with thoughts
of my long lost years.

Consciousness of a
great loss starts gnawing
my confidence like a
calculated woodpecker.
I feel like throwing away
my worthless creative pen
into the abysmal gutter.

Something Personal

When I would have
turned into only a name,
in the book of genealogy
of my great grandchildren;
when this not even five feet
body of mine would have
left behind no pulsating trace,
will there be something,
something exclusively mine,
delinked from parents and
siblings, husband and a
long line descendants ?

Something which will remind
those who will come after me
that there was somebody
called Sulekha ?

Will I be able to leave behind
something like Keats' Grecian Urn
before my dusty body is trampled
by a thousand feet ?

The Pampered Child

Your childlike pranks
are more endearing to me
than your artful articulations.

I know a man
nearing eighty, grows
as much naughty as
a boy of eight.
Full of mischief.
Volatile like a
sunset sky.

Your elfin eyes betray
no suspicious secrets.
Your taunting tales
can't compel me to label
your behavior
as shenanigans.

Who can understand you
better than the beloved
who loves you with the
heart of pampering Yashoda,
unlike possessive Radha !!

Come with Your Azure Being

The anguished Mother Earth
is waiting impatiently
to witness your awesome
final Dance of Death on
each expanded evil hood of
the heinous Hydra
loitering in the lanes
and bylanes of her
pious Yamuna like veins.

The fangs of human heart
have become more venomous than
the teeth of legendary snake Kaliya.
His scheming mind forever
engaged in designing and achieving
pernicious modus operandi.
His dark devilish soul
working like a bonded labourer
under Mephistopheles.

O' the Lotus eyed God,
for once come with
your azure being to
plunder the pestilential miasma.
The alluring Mother Earth
is waiting expectantly to listen
to your charismatic,

captivating ethereal song
floating through
a fragrant air with
the melodious tune
of your ecstatic flute.

Magnanimous Pole Star

You were the eternal Sun,
You were the pole star
of our family galaxy.
In family gatherings where
thousands throng and distant relatives
are at a loss to decide who is who;
everyone used to refer to your name.
And accordingly the relationships
were falling into places
to the pleasure of one and all.

You were the pole star,
the firm anchor of a huge family
uniting all in a thread of caring bondage
with your innocent, childlike, loving smile.

You were the pole star of
your political lineage whose members
loved and respected you
cutting across their political affiliations.
Your unblemished personality was
and is still now the ideal of many
surpassed by a few.

Time played havoc with your wonderful mind
taking away your brilliant memory,
Such a surprising memory of

people and places;
and you couldn't recognise me
when I met you for the last time.

In relationship you were a brother.
But were actually a father figure for me.
Loved, respected and admired;
Feared also with apprehensions of
committing mistakes and getting
admonishment, which of course
you never used to give.
I don't remember you ever getting angry
with me or anyone else except that day,
in Delhi when I returned home late
in the night after a visit to Taj Mahal
with my younger sister.
I knew that was not anger but
expression of your love and
concern for our safety.

Dear Rabi Bhai,
Forgive me from your heavenly abode
for my dereliction of duty towards you
which was never intentional
but sadly circumstantial.

May your magnanimous soul
rest in eternal peace and
may you shower your blessings
on all of us eternally.
(Composed on the first death anniversary of Sj. Rabi Ray, former Speaker of Lok Sabha, who left for his heavenly abode on 6th March 2017.)

My Happiness

Never do I
prefer to go on
a shopping spree
to buy happiness
at the cost of
someone's sorrow.

Bartering my jubilation
with someone's frustration.

There is
no dearth of
dishonest businessmen
selling adulterated delight
in glittering packages
with branded names.
Savouring such
ready-made rapture
is like inviting cancer.

My happiness is
simple and sustainable
a homemade cake
prepared by my own labour,
seasoned with condiments
like honesty and integrity
with an icing of honour.

Magic of Malati

Like a loving wife
the Malati creeper
rests her head on
the sturdy shoulders
of tall Champak tree,
mixing her honeyed aroma with
Champak's holy fragrance.

From evening
to early morning,
the air gets permeated
with an exotic sweet perfume
dispelling all depressive feelings.

Sniffing a whiff of
this sugary scent, often
acts as a magical medicine
and benevolent Nature has
blessed me with many
such marvellous moorings.

Forget Me

From your
conscious mind and
unconscious thoughts
remove me as soon as
the presence is felt.
Much before any
intrusion into your heart.

Each footprint
of an uninvited
destructive cyclone,
that brought
much devastation,
should be wiped clean.
All traces must be
swept away.

A mistake was committed.
Not easy to be rectified.
But repetition is unpardonable.

Our brief encounter
not a rendezvous
was a dream or
a daydream or
a terrible nightmare;

was an exploration
without destination.

Forget me
and if possible
forgive me.

Entice Me Not

This is not
the place where
the flowers of my love
can take colours and
bloom with cheers.

The blackish clouds
sailing in the azure sky,
The iridescent lights
coming from the setting sun
hold no fascination for me.

For me the birds' song
rings no note of pleasure,
The music of dropping rain
falls on my deaf ears.
The rainbow seems
sickening and distressing,
the petrichor is nauseating.

Take me to that land
where Aurora Borealis
is spread in the midnight.
The flower of my pure love
Lilies would bloom there
taking icy cold white colour
from the vast expanse of snow;

Sunflowers would merrily toss
their heads, fixing their gaze
on the never setting sun.

My love is
pure and platonic;
entice me not
with sensual desires
that turns me
into a phobic.

My Earnest Desires

My heart pines
for hours long meeting
with a secluded sea shore,
when the golden rays of
the setting sun would be
dancing on the waves like
a long tunnel of burning logs.

My heart yearns
for a rarefied morning walk,
an aimless roaming in a
reclining valley filled with
wild colourful flowers;
when the breeze would bring
their sweet aroma and touch
my body with misty grass.

My mind desires to befriend
uninterrupted loneliness,
days of undisturbed silence;
where the seeds of my creativity
could germinate and grow
unfettered by unwanted presence.

My tired mortal frame
craves no earthly pleasures
but prays for some peaceful rest

to rejuvenate and invigorate
for garnering enough strength to
fight the unending battle of life.

My soul hankers
after a reunion with
my true soul mate, my God
who would liberate me soon
from this meaningless
mundane existence.

Mysterious Pulchritude

Seven decades ago
on this day of October
a constellation of stars
conspired to curse
a baby going to be born,
as the Providence was planning
to play pranks on the mysterious
pulchritude of this baby's life.

A puffy girl child saw
the light of this earth just
a couple of days before the
holy arrival of goddess Durga.
Not to be blessed by her but to
carry the fighting spirit of goddess,
to become a bellicose baby.

Like a Tantalus she lived immersed
in a deluding pool of apparent
happiness, prosperity and success.
The water of achievements was
always receding back from her lips,
making her perennially thirsty and bitter.

Her hubris she failed to acknowledge,
her deprivations she took as a challenge,
her sorrows she gulped with a giggle.

Excruciating physical pain
was her faithful companion,
Agonizing, never-ending mental torture
was her constant consort, turning
her sometimes into a schizophrenic.

A puppet in everyone's hand,
she knew not how to say 'no'.
Her ungrudging shoulders became a
convenient ladder for others to climb up.

Ever reluctant to hurt others
she blinked back her tears bravely
when selfish, unsympathetic souls
continued to jeer at her and
poke her with pointed pins.

Encircled by crowds of people,
she lived a lonely life with
an endless enclosure standing
steadfast around her.

Blessed with no
enviable beauty or bounty,
her desolate life was lamentable.
Yet for no obvious reasons some
people become green eyed.
Her plain looks and artless articulations
made her the cynosure of some others.

Constantly bombarded and
devastated like Hiroshima
by jealous enemies, her

spirit remained undaunted.
She built herself afresh
after each destruction.
Years long suffering had
taught her the art of joining
broken pieces of life into
a colourful artistic mosaic.

The barbed bed of her life
caused much bloodshed
but enabled her to
remain awake forever.
A born fighter who disliked
easy defeat, she wallowed
in war of life with a firm
faith in God and Nature.

A Sanctum of Knowledge

A sanctum of knowledge,
professed guardian angel of
egalitarianism and socialism
is sanctified by the ruling power.
Students from far off lands
and different corners of the country,
come flying with wings of colourful hope.
To be moulded into magnificent
idols for others to follow
their indelible footprints.

Soon they are swallowed
by this illustrious institution
with a gargantuan appetite.
Soon the sanctum sells
the souls of these unsuspecting
youths to Machiavellian merchants.

Brainwashed to flock together
under a bloody banner,
they slowly turn into termites.
While their body is nourished by taxpayers,
their mind is engaged with suspicious scheming
of organizations rooted in enemy lands.

Pursuit of knowledge is
promptly prevented.

In the furnace of their minds
a fire is incessantly fueled.
Spirit of calculated rebellion
is clandestinely cultivated.

No Socrates or Aristotle or Einstein
is born out of this pyre of conspiracy
but only Machiavelli and Mephistopheles.

The termites use all their might
to dig a big hollow in the
trunk of the banyan tree,
that has stood the test of time
for thousands of years.

These red ants are bereft of true
aspirations without a soul of Valmiki.

The Soul of My Country

The Soul of my country
lives in all those ancient places,
in thousands of years old temples,
where culture and traditions are
not some insignificant pages of history.

The Soul of my country
is throbbing in the hearts of
innumerable god gifted children
who are born in twenty first century.
but speak a strange language of mystery.

The Soul of my country
is coursing through the veins of
staunch sons and dedicated daughters
whose only mission in life is to
protect the motherland and
safeguard its proud glory.

The Soul of my country
is not a dead topic for debate
nor a baseless idea to be laughed at,
But is the master craftsman of human kind
perennially going on weaving a love tapestry.

Black Eagle Books

www.blackeaglebooks.org
info@blackeaglebooks.org

Black Eagle Books, an independent publisher, was founded as a nonprofit organization in April, 2019. It is our mission to connect and engage the Indian diaspora and the world at large with the best of works of world literature published on a collaborative platform, with special emphasis on foregrounding Contemporary Classics and New Writing.

www.ingramcontent.com/pod-product-compliance
Lightning Source LLC
Chambersburg PA
CBHW060618080526
44585CB00013B/882